HERBIVORES
John Willis
EYEDISCOVER

Go to **www.eyediscover.com** and enter this book's unique code.

BOOK CODE

AVH87955

EYEDISCOVER brings you optic readalongs that support active learning.

Published by AV² by Weigl
350 5th Avenue, 59th Floor New York, NY 10118
Website: www.eyediscover.com

Copyright ©2019 AV² by Weigl
All rights reserved. No part of this publication may be reproduced, stored in a retrieval system, or transmitted in any form or by any means, electronic, mechanical, photocopying, recording, or otherwise, without the prior written permission of the publisher.

Library of Congress Control Number: 2018954184

ISBN 978-1-4896-8021-1 (hardcover)

Printed in the United States of America
in Brainerd, Minnesota
1 2 3 4 5 6 7 8 9 0 22 21 20 19 18

082018
120917

Project Coordinator: John Willis
Designer: Mandy Christiansen

Weigl acknowledges Alamy, Getty, iStock, and Minden Pictures as the primary image suppliers for this title.

EYEDISCOVER provides enriched content, optimized for tablet use, that supplements and complements this book. EYEDISCOVER books strive to create inspired learning and engage young minds in a total learning experience.

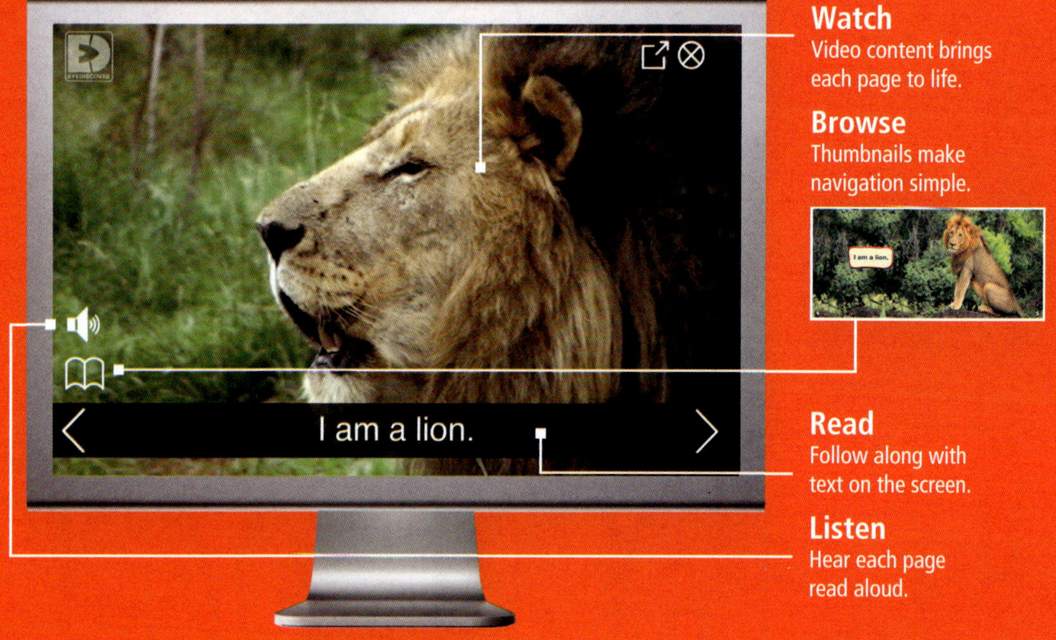

Watch
Video content brings each page to life.

Browse
Thumbnails make navigation simple.

Read
Follow along with text on the screen.

Listen
Hear each page read aloud.

Your EYEDISCOVER Optic Readalongs come alive with...

Audio
Listen to the entire book read aloud.

Video
High resolution videos turn each spread into an optic readalong.

OPTIMIZED FOR

- ✓ TABLETS
- ✓ WHITEBOARDS
- ✓ COMPUTERS
- ✓ AND MUCH MORE!

HERBIVORES

In this book, you will learn about

- what they are
- how they look
- what they eat

and much more!

Deer are animals that only eat plants. This means that they are herbivores.

6

Herbivores can be small. Many kinds of ants eat plants.

Some of Earth's biggest animals eat plants. Elephants are the largest herbivores.

Herbivores may eat leaves high in trees. Giraffes use their long necks to reach food.

Other herbivores eat plants from the water. Marine iguanas eat algae.

Some herbivores eat just one plant. Koalas can only eat leaves from one kind of tree.

Other herbivores eat many different foods. Goats eat leaves, roots, flowers, and seeds.

Beavers can eat tree bark. They cut down trees to get their food.

It is important to make sure we leave enough plants for herbivores to eat.

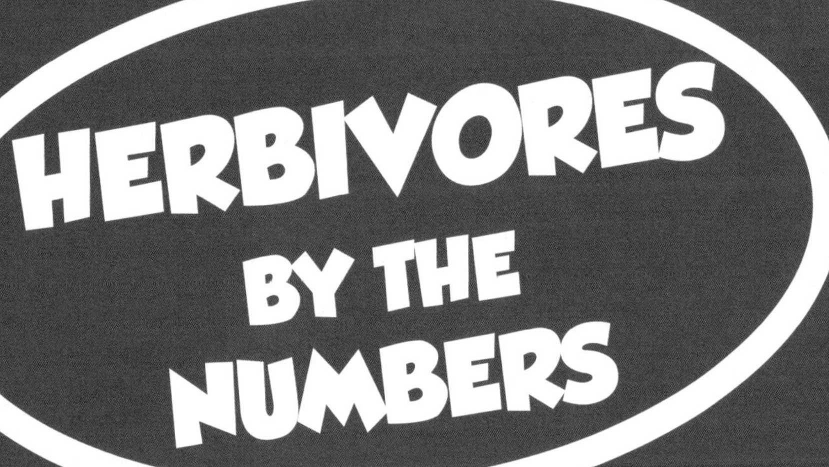

HERBIVORES BY THE NUMBERS

A giraffe's **neck** is about **6 feet** long. (1.8 meters)

Leafcutter ants eat about **20 percent** of South America's **leaves** each year.

An **elephant** can spend up to **18** hours eating **each day.**

Koalas eat **2.2** pounds of leaves **each day.**
(1 kilogram)

A goat's **stomach** is made of four different **chambers.**

Marine iguanas are the **only** lizards that spend **most** of their time in the **ocean.**

KEY WORDS

Research has shown that as much as 65 percent of all written material published in English is made up of 300 words. These 300 words cannot be taught using pictures or learned by sounding them out. They must be recognized by sight. This book contains 44 common sight words to help young readers improve their reading fluency and comprehension. This book also teaches young readers several important content words, such as proper nouns. These words are paired with pictures to aid in learning and improve understanding.

Page	Sight Words First Appearance
4	animals, are, eat, means, only, plants, that, they, this
7	be, can, kinds, many, of, small
8	Earth, some, the
10	food, high, in, leaves, long, may, their, to, trees, use
12	from, other, water
14	just, one
16	and, different
18	cut, down, get
21	enough, important, is, it, make, we

Page	Content Words First Appearance
4	deer, herbivores
7	ants
8	elephants
10	giraffes, necks
12	algae, marine iguanas
14	koalas
16	flowers, goats, roots, seeds
18	bark, beavers

Watch
Video content brings each page to life.

Browse
Thumbnails make navigation simple.

Read
Follow along with text on the screen.

Listen
Hear each page read aloud.

Go to www.eyediscover.com and enter this book's unique code.

BOOK CODE

AVH87955